Internet Marketing For Network Marketers

How To Create Automated Systems To Get Recruits and Customers Online

By Argena Olivis

www.networkmarketingkingdom.com

Bonus Video: How to Get Leads and Customers Online

Subscribe to Get Free Tips On How To Generate Leads and Get Customers

When you subscribe to get network marketing tips via email, you will get free access to exclusive subscriber-only resources. All you have to do is enter your email address to the right to get instant access.

These resources will help you get more out of your business – to be able to reach your goals, have more motivation, be at your best, and live the life you've always dreamed of. I'm always adding new resources, which you will be notified of as a subscriber. These will help you get an endless amount of leads and customers.

**Visit
www.networkmarketingkingdom.com/video
to Access The Bonus Video**

Table of Contents

Introduction

I want to thank you and congratulate you for reading the book, *"Internet Marketing for Network Marketers: How To Create Automated Systems To Get Recruits And Customers Online"*.

This book contains proven steps and strategies on how to create online systems that will allow you to get new leads and customers online.

In this book, you will discover the website creation strategy that will allow you to generate leads and customers online, even while you sleep.

I teach you the in-depth process on how to create a

website step by step that is geared toward getting customers online, recruits online, or both.

Traditional offline network marketing can be completely replaced with the methods you are about to learn.

Email marketing is the number one way to build relationships with prospects. Learn how collecting email addresses for a targeted audience will allow you to increase your online sales and customers.

Social media marketing is a great way to build trust and add value to your community. Many network markers don't realize how to use social media the right way and are spamming a lot of channels.

Learn how to use Facebook, Instagram, YouTube, Twitter, and Pinterest in a way that will allow you to generate endless leads online.

Find out how adding value and building an online community will make you more money rather than constantly promoting your company on social networks.

Learn how to make money with affiliate marketing and network marketing at the same time. Affiliate marketing is a great strategy that a lot of network marketers aren't using, but you should use it because not everyone will join your team, but they may purchase something that you recommend if you add enough value to their lives.

Use these proven strategies to increase your income online.

Make money online from more than just your network marketing company.

Learn how creating automated systems online can bring you more money than your company.

Make money from those who won't ever join your team by diversifying your income.

Lastly, you will learn the skills that you need to focus on so you know that you're doing the right thing at all times when promoting your business online.

Learn the income producing activities for both network marketing and internet marketing so you'll always be focused, and have the ability to leverage your time.

The truth is, you can build a team and get customers both on and offline. Why not focus your efforts online so you'll be able to live a life of freedom.

This book will show you how to set up systems so that you will no longer have to trade time for money.

Don't wait any longer, don't be one of those network marketers who procrastinate because they're afraid of success. Take action right now and start reading this book.

Why I Wrote This Book

I wrote this book because I know how it is to struggle to try to build a team and get customers the traditional way. Although this did work, I started to realize that it wasn't for me.

I've always studied network marketing, so when I saw that many top leaders are building their teams exclusively online- I wanted a piece of the pie.

You know how I know that you can build your network marketing company online? Because there are network marketing companies that are exclusively online. No door to door, no vendor events, and the only way you'd be able to sign up is online.

With technology today, you're able to build a team worldwide and never have to deliver an order.

Although online cannot and will not ever replace the connection people have from meeting face to face, it still works and it's worth working toward.

After about a year of being in my company, I decided to go exclusively online and I saw how it is possible to do. That's why I wrote this book, to share with you non-traditional methods that can help grow your business online.

Because I know what it's like to deliver orders. I know what it's like to set up at a vendor show and no one buys from me. I know what it's like to have team meetings and no one show up. I've been there, and I want you to take action and start building your business online so you can set boundaries with your time, and have some freedom in your life.

Thanks again for reading *Internet Marketing For Network Marketers*, I hope you enjoy it!

Chapter 1: Website Creation Strategy

Creating a website is the first thing you'll need to do in order to take your business online. If you truly want to create a business that works 24/7, no matter if you're there or not, you will need a website.

Creating a website is actually quite simple, but it's the upkeep and consistency that will determine your success in the end.

Just like building a company offline, online will take work-- maybe, even more, work. But that's just in the beginning.

By setting up a website to bring you leads all day, you will be ahead of most people in the industry.

To get even further ahead, you will need to constantly add valuable content to your website which will, in turn, help build your team or get you more customers.

What Will Your Website Be About

As a network marketer, your website's subject will depend on what you're trying to do. Would you like to generate leads or customers?

You can always go back and create another website, but for now think about what you want to focus on.

The thing about success is you have to focus. What is the one thing that will bring you closer to your goal right now?

Is it having customers so you can have "right now money" and share the results which in turn will help to bring in more recruits?

Or is it bringing in more recruits, which in turn will define you as a leader and attract even more recruits?

Creating A Website To Get Customers

Building a website to generate customers will be simple but you need to know some basic things.

Do not use your company's name on your website. This is for two reasons: 1) it's most likely against your company's guidelines 2) You want to brand yourself in order to build trust with the leads that come in.

On this website, you'll be creating content that has to do with your company's products. For example, if your company sells shoes. You want to create pages that help people with making shoe selections, finding the right shoe, finding quality shoes, etc.

All the content on your website will be centered around one subject.

This is called a "niche site". A niche site is when you focus on one particular subject and create content around it.

If your content is valuable and helps the customer out, they will want to buy from you. This is when you can send them over to your company website where they'll make their purchases. More on this later.

Creating A Website To Get Recruits

Creating a site for recruits will be similar to creating a website for customers.

Again, make sure not to mention your company's name. You will be branding yourself.

Branding yourself is when you're using your name and not your company's name while providing value through your website content.

You don't want to mention your company's name because they are already branded. You want leads to join your team because of you.

Anyone can join a company, people will only stick around if they see you as a person that can help them get what they want.

You'll be creating content that helps other network marketers. Think about the problems other network marketers just like you are having and solve them.

Once you do this you will create trust and be looked at as the "go to person" for network marketing.

In turn, they will either want to join your team or buy any information products and training you may have. More on information product creation later.

There is also an alternative for this if you truly want more targeted leads. You can create a website that is focused helping people in your particular company.

So when people search for more information about your company, you will have a site that has all the information they were looking for.

Leads will feel they have an advantage by joining your team because the content you've created for them is valuable and you look like you know what you're doing.

Why You Shouldn't Create A Website For Free

There are many sites out there like blogger.com and wordpress.com that allow you to set up an account and create a website for free.

I'm against these types of sites for many reasons.

The first reason is professionalism. Creating a website that ends with .wordpress or .blogger will look unprofessional.

People will take you and your business more seriously when you use a domain name that ends in .com

Also, if you go with those free sites you will not own your content. Whoever hosts your site will.

You also won't be able to monetize it the way you want to. Many of those sites have restrictions against things such as affiliate links and your own ads.

If you're not serious, and you're just dabbling in network marketing then you can create one of these websites. Just keep in mind that you will be giving up all control.

There are many benefits to using trustworthy hosting companies. You get customer support and you can create unlimited websites. This means you won't have to buy more hosting in order to create another site.

How To Create A Website

Now we're going to go into how to create an actual website. If you already own a website or blog you can move onto the next section.

Domain Name Rules

A domain name is the web address you type into a browser in order to get to a website. For example Google.com is a domain name.

There are a few rules you need to follow when naming your website.

1) Your domain name should have relevant keywords on what your site will be about

2) Avoid using your company name

3) Make sure to use .com

4) Avoid using dashes

5) Should be short and easy to remember

Registering A Domain Name

If you buy hosting first, sometimes you'll be able to get a free domain name with the host you choose.

I buy all my domain names from Godaddy because it allows for all of them to be in one place. You'll learn more about why you may want more than one domain name in later chapters.

Also, if you ever want to switch your hosting for any reason, you will not have to worry about transferring your domain name.

Transferring a domain name from one host to another can take up to three months.

To avoid all of this just register your domain name with Godaddy so if you ever want to change your host or use the domain name for something else you can easily just go in and do it.

Register you domain name in Godaddy by going to www.Godaddy.com and typing in the domain name you came up with of in the search box. Make sure to use the guidelines mentioned above.

If your first possible domain name is taken think of another one, keep trying until you find one that sounds right, looks right and works for you.

Make sure you buy a .com because this is the most universal ending for domain names and you will not encounter any trouble by using this.

Tip: To get the best price on your domain name search Google for "Godaddy Promo Codes"

Set Up Hosting

Next, you need to decide who you want to host your website. There are many options to go with. There are a ton of hosts you can use.

Find out which is best for you, make sure first that the host offers a platform that you can easily set up WordPress.

I use a company called Bluehost. To buy hosting with them go to Bluehost.com. I recommend them because they have outstanding customer service and you can easily set up WordPress.

After finding a host, install WordPress and you're good to go.

***For a complete tutorial on how to set up your website visit www.networkmarketingkingdom.com/website ***

The Website Creation Strategy

Now that you've registered your domain, you've set up WordPress, you're ready to start creating content.

The content you create is what will constantly bring leads into your funnel so you can turn them into customers and recruits.

The goal here is to create content related to your particular product if you're trying to reach customers, or your knowledge of the industry if you're trying to get recruits.

Really find your niche. For example: If your product is related to makeup you can create a website with content about makeup tips, tutorials, product reviews, etc.

Avoid using your company name. Before you create any

pages make sure you use Google Keywords Tool to find keywords to use in your pages that are not too high in competition and not too low.

There are also paid tools that can help with your keyword research and finding keywords that people are searching for. This may be worth it if you want to do in-depth research or find keywords and competition.

This will allow your site to rank high in Google. Use search engine optimization (SEO) to get found for different words and phrases so you can drive traffic to your site.

My favorite Wordpress plugin to use for this is Wordpress SEO Yoast. SEO Yoast shows you how to optimize your pages and posts for the search engines.

As you can see, internet marketing is a huge learning curve. There is so much to learn, it is a lot of work.

Your website's keywords are only one way you will get traffic to your website, though. You will also get traffic from email and social media marketing. More on that later.

Traffic is very important. There are different ways to get traffic and you want to expose your site to as many people as possible.

The equation is simple. More traffic=More leads.

The thing that will make you successful at creating a website that stands out is that you have to create content for a very targeted audience. The content you create has to teach someone how to do something.

When teaching others how to do something, make sure if they follow your blueprint that they'll get results.

After getting results from using your free content, they'll become raving fans and buy any product or service you have to offer in the future.

Raise your standards when it comes to creating your content. Do the research that is necessary and don't be lazy about it.

If you truly put everything into your website you will stand out from all other marketers trying to do the exact same thing. In turn, people will become attracted to you because you will be known as an expert in whatever you're teaching about.

The websites that do best are the ones that teach someone how to do something.

Keep in mind that you can easily create more than one website. If you use a host that allows you to have unlimited domains, you can create lots of websites and only pay for hosting once a year. To create a new site all you'd have to do is buy a new domain name.

So you'll be able to create sites for recruiting, getting customers, and possibly one for your team.

As long as you're creating lots of content that are valuable and use the proper keywords, you will generate traffic.

You may be wondering why I don't suggest you create a blog. This is because a blog will constantly have to be updated.

You want a static website that allows you to create something once and leave everything else up to the automated system.

So make sure the content you create is evergreen and not about events or subjects that are time dependent. If you create content that is not evergreen you can use it in your social media updates.

Creating A Team Site

Creating a team site is the best way to leverage your time. If you put out valuable content on another website or through other channels such as social media or email then people will want to join your team.

People will also want to join your team once they see your professionalism you have by having a dedicated team site. The best way to get more team members is to get results and share results. In turn, this will attract others and they'll want to do what you're doing.

Make your team site a membership site exclusive only to your team members. Here you can walk them step-by-step through the process after they sign up to join your team.

You can also offer them training and everything they need to be successful on your team.

This will allow you to leverage your time. You will not have to answer the same questions over and over again. If you put everything you would say to a new team member on that site you will save them time and you time.

Chapter 2: Email Marketing

Email marketing is the way you will capture leads that visit your website or squeeze page. It's also a way to get traffic back to your website.

To capture the names and emails of your prospects you will need email software. The most popular is Aweber, this is what I use.

Once you buy the software you can place an opt-in box on your website so that visitors can enter their name and email.

The leads you collect from your website are yours to keep no matter what happens. If something happens to your website-- you'll always have your list to refer back to.

This is the importance of creating a list. A list can also be profitable and can allow you to send emails without having to actively type them out each time you want to send one out.

This is where the automated system comes in. In Aweber, you can create a series of follow-up messages that will go out to your email list. You can schedule them to go out whenever you want.

These email autoresponders will take you out of the equation so you can work on other things that are income producing activities-- like making phone calls to leads about your company, showing leads your presentation, and following up.

Or, if you ever decide to take your business online, you can live a freedom lifestyle where you have systems set up that you're earning from so you can live the life you want.

You will also have leads calling you about your company instead of having to call them.

Set up and send out autoresponders messages that help your target audience, bring them back to your website, and puts them in a position to want to buy what you're selling or join your team.

Set up about 10 autoresponders to start off with. Send them out about every other day.

How To Get Leads To Opt In

People are not going to just come to your website and enter their email address and name unless you're offering them something of value.

Keep in mind that your audience is most likely already getting tons of emails a day and they do not want any more spam coming into their inbox.

So make sure the messages you send out are quality and helpful.

Types Of Emails You May Send To Your List:

- new blog post

- new product

- new podcast episode

- sale on a product

- new video

- free product

- etc.

Always have a good reason to email your list, if you have something of value to share, send them an email.

Create an Opt-In Offer to Get Leads on Your List

An opt-in offer is something you create that you give your visitors for free that will make them want to get on your email list.

Make your opt-in offer something relevant to what your target audience will want.

Some ideas: Free course, eBook, guide, free report, audio, conference call, interview with an expert, free consultation...

Whatever you decide to give away will be digital. Try to make it something that is independent of your time so that you don't have to be there to deliver it.

After your offer is created, get the link to it and put it in the first autoresponder message that is sent out immediately when a lead opts-in.

This allows you to give them something of value for free without having to be there. Which in turn builds trust and likeability.

The follow-up messages you create after that should be related to your target audience and the information on your website.

Create a new email list when necessary. A new list is necessary if you want to create an audience for another website you have, or when you want to target a different audience.

By creating an email list you, in turn, will get traffic back to your website or straight back to your company website so leads can either buy from you or join your team. All of this will be on autopilot.

Broadcast Messages

Most email software allows you to send out broadcast messages to your list.

Above we talked about autoresponders, but a broadcast message may be necessary depending on the message you're sending out.

For example, if you have a sale on your product or a special offer that is only for a limited time, you want to send out a broadcast message.

If you're worried about people getting more than one email from you in a day, make sure to schedule your autoresponders on certain days so you can send broadcast messages on particular days.

This may not be automated, but it's a great way to keep your list updated on new information such as events, sales, and promotions.

The Takeaway

Email marketing will be the way you make most of your money through online marketing overall. People check their email daily, and for a lot of people it's what they do as soon as they wake up in the morning.

Keep in mind that there's a lot of competition out there so treat your list like gold. Only send them emails that will further their business or save them some money.

Make sure to always keep a backup of your list. It's your biggest asset. If you haven't started email marketing and you want to build your network marketing business online-- the best time to get started building a list was yesterday.

If you don't learn anything from this book, learn that email marketing is the way of the future. And it can be the difference between becoming a top earner and losing everything you've worked hard to build online.

I have a **free video** on how to get started with email marketing. You can check it out by visiting:

http://www.argenaolivis.com/email-marketing-101/

In this training, I walk you through how to set up your opt-in offer and create autoresponder messages.

Chapter 3: Social Media Marketing

Social media marketing is another way that you can generate leads and customers online. It's also a way to get traffic back to your website or squeeze page/email list.

I'm going to go over the most popular social media sites: Facebook, Instagram, Twitter, Pinterest, and YouTube.

Make sure that you're only focusing on one or two social media sites at a time. It's okay to create profiles for each site, but make sure you're only giving your attention to one or two.

I say this because you want to master one form of social media before moving on to the next. Building your business online will take extreme focus and consistency.

Make sure to measure your results. If you see you're getting more results from one site, then focus on that one site. Don't spread yourself too thin. **Learn everything you can about one of these social media channels and give it all you've got.**

Facebook

Facebook is a way for you to market your business. Use Facebook to get leads online. Create a Facebook Fan Page.

Share quality tips and content with your Facebook fans. Facebook is a way to build a community of trusted and loyal fans.

Use Facebook to get more email subscribers. Tell your fans about the email offer you've created in order to get them on your list. You can post about your optin offer and create a page app for it (page apps are only seen by desktop users).

Share tips and content that you've written on your website, new videos, new podcasts, webinars, conference calls, etc. Also, share any news and events you have and promotions your company may be having.

Share Results

Sharing results will allow you to inspire others and ultimately strike curiosity about what exactly you're doing.

Make sure to post when a new team member joins your team. Have their picture and also, tag them in the post. This will make the team member feel special and also make you look like an authority.

Share when you get a big bonus or when something amazing happens. Whenever you get extraordinary monetary rewards from your company share it on your fan page. This shows your hard work and it also inspires others.

It lets other see what's possible. It also makes you look like you know what you're doing. And if you look like you know what you're doing, people will think you can help them to achieve the same results.

Don't just post about your company or product. People love to see things like lifestyle images and really get to know you.

Connect on a deeper level with your fans. Ask questions and share resources with them that have been helpful to you.

Update your page about 8-10 times a day. Preferably once every hour.

To automate this you can use a tool like Hootsuite. Or you can schedule posts directly from your Facebook page because Facebook has a scheduler.

Instagram

Instagram is a great way to capture leads. Use hashtags a lot. Here are my favorites:

#entrepreneur #internetmarketing #business #personaldevelopment #mlm #networkmarketing

Instagram is an app where you can share images or very short videos. Use images of your lifestyle and take screen shots of things you're working on.

Also, similar to Facebook make sure to post your results.

You can use apps to create images and share tips or quotes. My favorite apps to use for Instagram are word swag, textgram, or aviary.

Use whatever hashtags are relevant to your topic or to your particular post.

If you use a lot of great hashtags you won't have any problems getting followers and leads. You can direct message on Instagram too-- a lot of people don't know that.

Make sure you make the descriptions under your images enticing. Use emoji's and different symbols to stand out.

I don't know about you but I hate typing long descriptions directly from my phone, so I usually type the descriptions from my desktop and send it to myself via email. After that, I copy and paste the description into Instagram. I do the same for my hashtags.

Make sure you use screen shots when you want to showcase a product or service you offer. Screenshots is an easy way to show prospects what you're talking about.

You can schedule your Instagram posts by using postso.com to automate this. Instagram is the most difficult social media site to automate.

Twitter

Twitter is a great way to find out what people in the industry are up to because you can search for a specific phrase and see what people are posting in real time.

With Twitter, you can share simple tips and links because you are only allowed up to 140 characters per post.

You are able to call attention to others by using their twitter name in your posts.

It's also a great way to get a lot of exposure. You can do this by using hashtags for things that are trending.

The best way to automate your twitter is to link it to your Facebook page so that every time you post on Facebook the same post will appear in your Twitter feed.

If you're focusing more on Facebook this is a great way to automate things. But if you want to focus on Twitter, post to twitter individually from Facebook.

There are also schedulers you can use such as buffer app and Hootsuite. But if you want to automate, it's best to schedule your posts on Facebook and have your post on Facebook show up in your Twitter feed.

Just like Instagram, make sure to use relevant hashtags in your tweets.

Pinterest

Pinterest can be an amazing traffic source to your website.

Pinterest is a social media site that is similar to Instagram because it's image based.

So just like Instagram, make sure to post relevant pictures.

Some ideas include:

- screen shots of a new blog post

- quote images

- screen shots of projects you're working on

- screen shots of your information products

- screenshots of the products your company sells

- lifestyle images

The great thing about Pinterest is you can add videos. So when you make YouTube videos make sure to post them on Pinterest.

Some great free resources to make images are www.picmonkey.com and www.canva.com

Don't forget to use hashtags on Pinterest too! These will allow your images to be found and repined.

Pinterest has an audience of mainly women, and if you sell anything women can use--this can definitely be a source of traffic to you.

Make sure that you put a pin its button on the images on your website to make it easy for people to share.

Remember, more traffic=more leads.

You can use a tool such as www.curalate.com to automate your pins. Pinterest, like Instagram, is more difficult to automate.

YouTube

YouTube is one of the best channels to build trust with your audience and in turn, generate more leads online.

The thing about video is not everyone does it. Many people are afraid of what they will look like on camera or let things like not having a professional camera stop them.

If you post videos you will already be ahead of those who are too afraid to.

And keep in mind that you don't have to be in your videos. You can create training using PowerPoint presentations and record your computer screen and upload it as a video.

To record your screen you can use free software like Jing or Screen-Cast-O-Matic.

Video marketing is amazing and if you haven't, you should start making videos.

Videos can be time-consuming though, but there is a way to get around this and be more productive.

It's called video batching. What you do is create a list of topics for videos you want to create and record all the videos in one sitting. To come up with topics, use a something like Google AdWords Keywords Tool.

You can batch videos for the week or for the month depending on how often you want to post.

You can also turn this into an income stream by signing up for YouTube's partner program. This is where Google AdSense pays you a portion of what they are making from advertisements.

You can create a video and a blog post on the same topic and embed the video into your blog post, this will give your visitors the ultimate experience. The best way to save time and get the most out of this is to record your video and have it transcribed.

You can have your video transcribed for cheap by using outsourcing services such as Fiverr.com.

The visitors that love to watch video will be able to do so, and the ones who like to read will do so-- it's a win-win.

Another great thing about this is the ability to turn the audio from your YouTube video into a podcast.

Here's how it goes: video > audio/podcast> transcription/blog post> lead generation from multiple sources.

You will also be more easily found in the search engine if you use keywords that are being searched for and are not too competitive.

You can use programs like Windows Live Movie Maker to edit your videos. And you can go to Fiverr.com to get an intro. It all depends on how much time and effort you're willing to put into it.

As long as you have good lighting and sound, viewers will watch your videos if they are into what you are teaching or showing.

To save time, create a document of all the information you want to put in your video description. When you upload your videos in the future, copy and paste the document into your YouTube description.

Make sure to include a link back to your website. Mention your opt-in offer in order to get more people on your email list. Preferably have a link to your squeeze page as the first item in your description.

To automate this, YouTube has a scheduler inside of it that will post your videos for whatever time you want them released.

As you can see, video is a game changer, and can be critical to your success.

Keep in mind that YouTube is the second biggest search engine in the world, so you may want to get on there.

Chapter 4: Affiliate Marketing

Don't have your own training products yet? That's, fine. You don't need your own product to make extra income online.

You can make an extra stream of income in addition to your company by affiliate marketing.

Affiliate marketing is when you earn a commission on a product by someone clicking on a unique link provided to you by the owner of the product and buying the product through your unique link.

When you promote a product make sure it's relevant to your audience. Keep in mind that although you're an independent distributor through your company-- some of what you're doing may be similar to affiliate marketing because you are sending people to your online store so they can buy through you-- it's not much different.

But everyone may not be interested in buying your company's products or training. So if you feel that your audience (such as your email list) can truly benefit from a product, become an affiliate for it and recommend it to your audience.

In order to get people to buy through your affiliate link, you need to give them a reason. Tell them the benefits of the product or demonstrate how to use the product.

Do not recommend products that you haven't used yourself, if you do you won't be able to give an honest review of it.

It would be better if you could make a video demonstrating the product so people can see you, and see that you actually own it.

Some tricks for getting more affiliate sales:

- create bonuses for the people that buy through your link

- Buy domain names and set them up so they'll forward straight to the affiliate offer

- Give an honest review, no product is perfect so let them know what it lacked

Try to develop a relationship with the affiliate. They may do a special offer for your audience.

Many affiliates will give you email swipes and other tools to be successful. Take their advice and see what works best for promoting their offers.

Make sure to create an affiliate disclaimer/disclosure policy on your website. (FTC Disclaimer).

Do not try to sell too early and make sure what you're trying to sell is relevant to your audience.

Clickbank is the best place to find offers to promote. But there are tons of other channels like commission junction and share-a-sale.

The best way to find out if a company has an affiliate program is searching the company's name in Google and putting the words "affiliate program" at the end.

You can also check by going directly to their website and scrolling down to the bottom to see if they have a link for affiliates.

All in all, affiliate marketing done right is a way to make some extra money online in addition to your network marketing company.

Chapter 5: Diversify Your Income Online

Now that you are getting some income from selling your products online and getting residual income from the recruits you've brought on-- it's time to diversify your income.

You always want to have multiple streams of income coming in, just to be safe and also to make more money.

Keep in mind that you don't own your company and they can make changes at any time-- this can really influence your income.

So to avoid putting all your eggs in one basket, you may want to create other streams of income online.

Don't try to get into too many things too soon, though. You can work on things on a quarterly basis. You'll get the best results when you focus on one project at a time. So make sure you meet your income goal with one project before moving on to another.

Ads

If your website is getting at least 25+ visitors a day, consider putting up advertising.

I say wait until you get 25+ unique visitors a day because there is no point of applying for advertising if you don't have any traffic because you won't make any money.

The most popular ones are Google AdSense, Infolinks,

and Media.net

You place ads on your site and when a visitor clicks on them you get paid a percentage.

Make sure to never click on your own ads and don't tell anyone else to click them for you. Many of these programs are very strict and if you're not careful they can ban you for life.

Never make ads your only source of income. It's too risky.

Information Products

Another way to diversify your income is to create your own information products.

Information products are things like eBooks, audios, video courses (Udemy), etc.

Anything that can be created and sent out digitally is an information product.

Depending on how long you've been in network marketing you may already have some products you can put up for sale on your site.

You can sell audio like conference call recordings and team training.

You can also sell seats to webinars.

If you're more focused on getting customers rather than team building then you may want to consider creating an eBook around the product you sell.

You can also put your eBook up on Kindle and make an

income while still directing traffic to your website and growing your email list. Click here to get my free kindle book creation course.

You can consider creating a membership site or group that people have to pay to use. It could include network marketing training.

There are tons of products you can create, you just have to think big and take action. The money is there-- you just have to invest in your knowledge and share what you know works.

You do not have to be an expert to provide value. No information is really new, it's all recycled. But people may connect with you better or they may like the way you teach better than others.

Take what you've been learning and share it with the world. And turn your ideas into profit.

All in all, make sure that if you create a product that everything is automated. Don't create physical products if you truly want to work smarter.

Keep in mind that you will still have to work hard at first even if everything is automated. It takes consistency and motivation to get things set up and running smoothly.

But it's totally worth it, right?

Your product should be created once and independent of your time if you want to create passive income.

If you really want to expand your reach, put your digital product on Clickbank to reach more people. Others will become an affiliate for it and help you to sell it.

A customer should be able to purchase your product and pay for it and the money should be automatically sent to your bank account so you won't have to be there to for the transaction.

This process is easy to set up with programs like Ejunkie, Gumroad, and PayPal.

Chapter 6: Skills To Work On

Internet marketing and network marketing are both steep learning curves. Trying to learn both can be overwhelming.

Here are the skills you will need in order to succeed in both.

Personal Development

Personal development is the number one skill you need to focus on. Your mindset is truly important.

The person who is motivated and ready to work will always beat the person who is not sure of themselves or their possibilities.

If you procrastinate and don't take action, it's because of your mindset. As you learn new things and try to have a better life there will be many obstacles that come in your way.

Becoming a better person, in general, will increase your income dramatically.

So make sure you focus on staying motivated and working on your mindset.

Check out my book Network Marketing Mindset for encouragement and confidence building.

Adding Value

You are most likely into network marketing for one main reason-- to make more money. And there's nothing wrong with that.

But what you have to realize is you're truly going to have to have something of value to offer people if you want to make money online.

The more valuable you are, the more money you will make. When creating free information try not to hold anything back and really blow people away.

There is so much free information out there that you shouldn't be trying to keep secrets because someone somewhere is helping people get results by sharing everything they know and more.

If you have a product and you don't want to share everything out of respect for the people that have already paid for it. That's understandable. But make sure to try your best to help people get results with the free information you put out there.

Today there are millions of websites and products-- you have to be different.

They say that the amount of money you make is a direct correlation to how much value you create. So if you're not making any money, you should take a step back and see what you can improve on.

Don't hold anything back. **Be obsessed with your customers** and don't worry about competition. If you are consistent and truly want to help others then you're already ahead.

Invest in yourself. Then after you learn something and

get results from it-- teach it in your own way.

Copy Writing

This is a high paid skill that many people don't think to pursue and learn.

If you want to sell online, you're going to have to have a way with words.

This skill will come in handy with sales letters, descriptions, and emails.

SEO

Search engine optimization is another skill you may want to learn. Although there are plugins like SEO Yoast that help you, you still want to know how to use keywords so you can rank high in the search engines.

You may be consistent at creating content, but it's useless if no one sees it.

Content Syndication

Work smarter. Learn to re-purpose your content.

For example: Create a blog post on how to lose weight >create a video on how to lose weight > put that video on YouTube> embed that video into your blog post> tell others about your new blog post on Social media> Send that blog post to your email list

Here are other ways to re-purpose and syndicate content:

- Turn YouTube videos into audios and podcasts

- Turn a collection of blog posts into an eBook

- Turn blog posts into a power point presentation and put on Slideshare

- Turn videos into blog posts

- Use all the content from your website and turn it into a book

- Take a screen shot of your blog post and post on social media

There are many ways you can use your content to create other content.

Tracking Performance

Use tools such as Google Analytics and StatCounter to track your performance.

These tools will tell you where your traffic is coming from and what keywords are getting the most attention.

Also, create a spreadsheet in excel and track your social media engagement, affiliate sells, and other income over time.

See what's working and what's not working. Focus more on what's working and leave the other stuff behind.

Traffic

Learn the different sources where you can get traffic online. Focus on the top two things that are bringing you the most traffic.

Master your traffic sources and then move on to other sources to expand your reach.

Here is how it goes:
traffic>leads>conversions>sales>happy customer>shared experience>referrals> traffic

The Takeaway

If you want to truly maximize your business and profits, when your business starts to grow and you're making a sizeable income. It may be time to hire a virtual assistant that can help you with a lot of these tasks.

It's a lot of work to create and syndicate content. You're going to need help or you'll be working in your business, not on your business.

In time, you'll want to hire a team to handle customer service, social media updates, etc.

In the meantime, if you have the money outsource what you can be using services such as Fiverr.com and Odesk.com. There you can find someone to work for you for an affordable price.

I know that you have what it takes to be a successful internet network marketer. There's a lot of competition, but no one can replace you. Not everyone is working smart. And not everyone had the right mindset to keep pushing even when times get hard.

Good luck on your journey to development as a better person and a better marketer.

Your Feedback Is A Gift

Thank you again for reading *Internet Marketing For Network Marketers*!

I hope this book was able to help you to discover how to generate leads online.

The next step is to take action!

Finally, if you enjoyed *Internet Marketing for Network Marketers*, then I'd like to ask you for a favor, would you be kind enough to leave a review for this book on Amazon? It'd be greatly appreciated!

By reviewing this book, you'll give me feedback on what I can do better or if I've done a great job. It also helps others to find the book.

Thank you and good luck with everything!

Preview Of "How To Get Customers In Your Network Marketing Company"

Chapter 1: How To Generate Leads

Get Your Mindset Straight

Before we begin generating leads we need to make sure that you have the right mindset.

Network marketing is not an easy industry. But if you have a product you believe in, know in your heart and in your mind that you can be successful.

You have to be able to take rejection as a learning experience. If any of these strategies you take action on don't work for you, tweak them to make them work for you.

Your mindset has to be right. And you have to stay motivated and consistent to win.

Here are some tips on staying motivated daily:

- read for an hour a day (business or personal development books)

- watch YouTube videos on network marketing and motivation

- listen to business and network marketing

podcasts

- work out and eat healthily

- have a daily routine and schedule and stay consistent

- set goals and do the work

- make a to-do list every night before bed

- read positive affirmations in the mirror

- create a vision board

- put a note or picture of the lifestyle you want to live on your laptop

Those are just examples of how to stay motivated. Do all that are suggested to you, or just one. But make sure you're not wasting your precious time.

Once your mindset is right, you can start generating leads.

So, have you done some of the suggested motivators above? I hope so. Now you're ready to move on and start generating leads.

How To Generate Leads

The number one thing you have to remember is you

ALWAYS want to get contact information.

If you don't get a person's contact information, you just lost a lead and a customer.

There are many ways to get a lead's contact information both online and offline without being invasive....

Visit www.NetworkMarketingKingdom.com to check out the rest off How To Get Customers In Your Network Marketing Company

Check Out My Other Network Marketing Books

Below you'll find some of my other popular books that are popular on Amazon and Kindle as well. Alternatively, you can visit my <u>author page</u> on Amazon to see other work done by me.

<u>Network Marketing Mindset: Personal Development and Confidence Building For Network Marketers</u>

<u>How To Get Customers In Your Network Marketing Company: The Complete Guide To Converting Leads Into Loyal Customers</u>

<u>Network Marketing Selling Secrets: 50 Ways To Get More Customers Online and Offline</u>

<u>Network Marketing For Introverts: Guide To Success For The Shy Network Marketer</u>

Bonus Video: How to Get Leads and Customers Online

Subscribe to Get Free Tips On How To Generate Leads and Get Customers

When you subscribe to get network marketing tips via email, you will get free access to exclusive subscriber-only resources. All you have to do is enter your email address to the right to get instant access.

These resources will help you get more out of your business – to be able to reach your goals, have more motivation, be at your best, and live the life you've always dreamed of. I'm always adding new resources, which you will be notified of as a subscriber. These will help you get an endless amount of leads and customers.

**Visit
www.networkmarketingkingdom.com/video
to Access The Bonus Video**

About The Author

My name is Argena Olivis and I'm an internet marketer and serial entrepreneur. I began my network marketing in journey January 2013.

What originally attracted me to network marketing was the idea of passive and residual income. I also liked how it allowed me to get out of my shell and start to meet like-minded people.

I love network marketing because it builds confidence and it's one of the most challenging industries. I had a lot of success in finding and retaining customers in my previous network marketing company.

Recently I decided not to pursue network marketing as a career anymore but I still love teaching what I've learned during my journey. I now am focusing on my other businesses that include internet marketing. And I'm taking my love of finding and retaining customers and applying it to my other businesses.

The industry is great and it's always fun to see motivated entrepreneurs winning. I know you'll do well. And I wish you the best of luck in whatever you decide to pursue in the future.

www.ingramcontent.com/pod-product-compliance
Lightning Source LLC
Chambersburg PA
CBHW070959180526
45168CB00003B/1212